Natural Wonders

Robert Gogan

Series Editor
Jean McConochie

Regents Publishing
Company, Inc.
New York

To

my students

R.G.

Contents

About the Author

Robert Gogan teaches English as a second language (ESL) at Chamberlayne Junior College in Boston and at Harvard University in Cambridge. He has previously taught ESL at Northeastern University and the American Language Academy (Boston), at Nasson College (Springvale, Maine), and in Esfahan, Iran.

A graduate of Hampshire College in Amherst, Massachusetts, Mr. Gogan also holds a master of education degree from Boston University. He is the editor of MATSOL Newsletter, published by the Massachusetts affiliate of TESOL (Teachers of English to Speakers of Other Languages). *Natural Wonders* is his first book.

About the Series Editor

Jean McConochie is associate professor of English and coordinator of the English-as-a-second-language program at Pace University in New York City. Dr. McConochie has published two ESL texts—*Twentieth Century American Short Stories* and, with Alice H. Osman, *If You Feel Like Singing;* she has also contributed, as writer and editor, to a variety of professional publications.

A graduate of the University of Illinois and Teachers College, Columbia University, Dr. McConochie has taught both students and teachers of English as a second or foreign language at various universities in the United States as well as in France, Poland, Yugoslavia, and Canada.

To the Reader

Every part of the world has natural wonders. Natural wonders are beautiful places: mountains, rivers, waterfalls. People don't make them.

This book tells the stories of five natural wonders in the United States: Niagara Falls, the Grand Canyon, the Mississippi River, Yellowstone National Park, and Yosemite National Park.

Read about these wonders. Think about them. One day, you can visit them. They are here for you and me.

R. G.

To the Teacher

This book

The Regents Readers are written at six levels of difficulty. *Natural Wonders* (Level 1) uses a base vocabulary of 300 words with verbs in the present (both simple and continuous) and the *will* future. There are no comparative constructions; the only subordinate constructions are a few *because* clauses.

An additional 60 words are explained either in context or in a footnote. Each word is then repeated in the same chapter and in subsequent chapters. How much special vocabulary (such as *white water*) individuals remember will depend on their personal interests, as is true with any reading experience.

Each story in *Natural Wonders* is approximately 1,000 words long, providing an opportunity for sustained reading within a single frame of reference. The stories are divided into sub-sections of 100 to 150 words so that a student can read one section at a time with increasing comprehension for each successive section in a chapter. Pre-reading questions are intended both to stimulate the reader's curiosity and to establish the important habit of posing questions—and guessing their answers—before one begins to read. You will probably want to return to these questions for postreading discussion.

Exercises at the end of each chapter review aspects of the entire chapter and include references to previous chapters in the book. These exercises are intended to help students increase their reading power. The answer key provides immediate feedback, which is important in building reading skills. Illustrations are included both to give pleasure and to clarify meaning.

If students become interested in what they are reading and enjoy learning more about the world we live in, this book's purpose will have been realized.

The grading of this series

The thirty-six books in the Regents Readers series follow the structure and vocabulary guidelines of the two most comprehensive reference works available: L. G. Alexander, W. Stannard Allen, R. A. Close, and R. J. O'Neill, *English Grammatical Structure* (Longman Group Limited, 1975) and Roland Hindmarsh, *Cambridge English Lexicon* (Cambridge University Press, 1980), with modifications where British and American usage differ.

Series editor's acknowledgments

My personal thanks are due to O. Dean Gregory, who many years ago showed me how to write controlled reading materials; to Adrian du Plessis, who suggested the use of the Longman and Cambridge guides; to Louis Carrillo, who is both resourceful and unflappable; to Winifred Falcon, who gives understanding responses and honest reactions; and, most of all, to the many friends—old and new—who have devoted their considerable talents to writing this series.

J. McC.

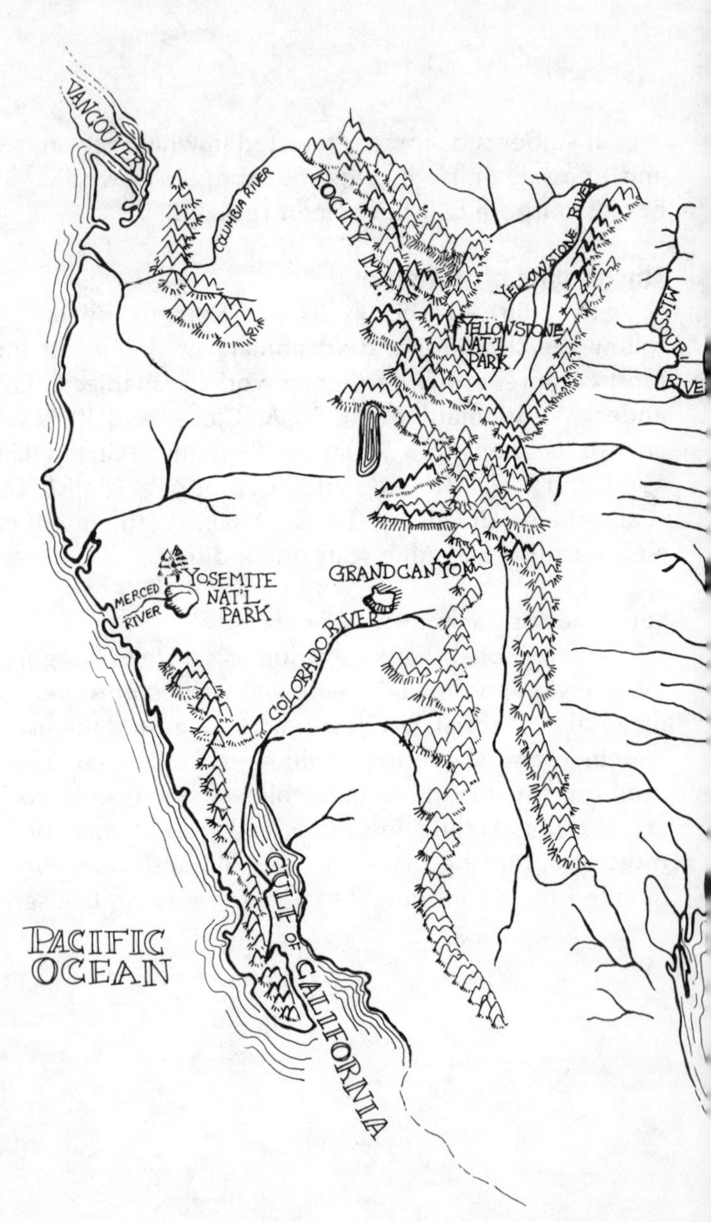

VANCOUVER
COLUMBIA RIVER
ROCKY MTS.
YELLOWSTONE RIVER
MISSOURI RIVER
YELLOWSTONE NAT'L PARK
GRAND CANYON
YOSEMITE NAT'L PARK
MERCED RIVER
COLORADO RIVER
GULF OF CALIFORNIA
PACIFIC OCEAN

Reference Map

Niagara Falls with U.S. in foreground, Canada in background. (Courtesy of the New York State Department of Commerce)

Niagara Falls: The Dangerous Beauty

What do you know about Niagara Falls?
Why is Niagara Falls beautiful?
Why are the falls dangerous?

1

There are five large **lakes** between the United States (the U.S.) and Canada. The water in these lakes is very deep and blue. Boats and ships can go 1,160 miles (1,867 kilometers) from west to east on these lakes. There is a river between two of the lakes. It is the Niagara River. But boats and ships do not go on this river. Why don't they?

Some rivers are brown. They are slow. Some rivers are blue. They are not slow, but they are not **fast**. Some rivers are white. They are very fast. The Niagara River is a white river. It is white because the water is fast and angry. It is **dangerous** for ships. But the fast, angry water is not the worst thing for them. The worst thing is Niagara Falls. Here the river becomes two big waterfalls. The water **falls** down, down, down.

---

lake - a large area of water with land all around it.
fast - quick, not slow.
dangerous - not safe. You must be careful in a dangerous place.
falls - goes down quickly.

On the American side, the water falls 167 feet (51 meters). It is a high waterfall. It is wide, too. On the American side, the falls are 1,060 feet (323 meters) wide. The Canadian Falls are high and wide, too. They are 158 feet (48 meters) high and 2,600 feet (792 meters) wide. Four big lakes push their water over these two waterfalls. Together, these waterfalls are called Niagara Falls.

Sometimes a boat or ship goes the wrong way. It goes over Niagara Falls. It breaks. Its pieces are very small. Most pieces are lost. Niagara Falls is not a good place for boats or ships!

2

People from every part of the world visit Niagara Falls. You can hear many languages. You can hear English, French, Spanish, Italian, Greek, Russian, Chinese, Japanese, and many other languages—languages from all over the world.

There are many ways to see Niagara Falls. They are all wet ways, because there is a lot of water in the air. You can stand beside the top of the waterfall; there the ground moves a little bit. You can walk behind the waterfall. But you must walk carefully; it is a narrow walkway. There you can see the sunshine through a water window. You can ride on a fast little ship called the **Maid of the Mist.** It goes on the milk-colored water under Niagara Falls. You can stand on the ground at the **bottom** of the waterfall; the ground moves there too.

Maid of the Mist - The name of a boat.
  maid - a young girl, maiden.
  mist - a cloud of very, very small drops of water in the air.
bottom - the lowest part.

The yellow sunshine makes a **rainbow**. There is a lot of mist in the air, so the sun doesn't need rain for this. At night, people shine strong lights on the waterfall: red, orange, yellow, green, blue. These lights make a night rainbow. The moon makes beautiful light for the waterfall too.

Maid of the Mist.
(Courtesy of the Niagara Falls Convention & Visitors Bureau)

---

rainbow - a bow, or arch, of seven colors. Sunshine through water makes a rainbow.

Niagara Falls in
winter. (Courtesy of
the New York State
Department of
Commerce)

3

People listen to Niagara Falls in the summer. The water's noise is very strong. You can hear it 20 miles (30 kilometers) away. You must speak into your friend's ear. He or she must listen to you very carefully. In the hotels near the waterfall, many people cannot sleep.

But in winter, the noise stops. It stops because the waterfall stops. The cold weather makes the waterfall an **ice** picture. You can speak very quietly and your friend can hear you.

Niagara Falls is beautiful in the summer. The weather then is very nice. It is not hot, because the water is cold and there is a lot of water in the air. Many people **get married** and then come here to see it. Every day you can see hundreds of new husbands and wives. Beside the beautiful waterfall, they think about their happy tomorrows.

---

ice - At 32° F (0° C), water becomes ice.
 ° - degree.   **F** - Fahrenheit.   **C** - Celsius.
get married - become husband and wife.

But some people are not happy. They want to die. These people come to Niagara Falls too. They jump into the Niagara River. They say goodby to the world. They go over the waterfall, and nobody sees them again.

4

Some people come to Niagara Falls because they like to do dangerous things. **Imagine** it is June 30, 1859. A man is walking across Niagara Falls on a very high **line**. The line is 1,300 feet (396 meters) long. It is 230 feet (70 meters) over the water! The line goes from the Canadian side of the waterfall to the U.S. side.

The man's name is Jean Blondin. He is from France. A big crowd is watching this Frenchman. Some English people are here with the son of the king of England. Many Canadian people are here. And many people from the U.S. are here. Everybody is watching Jean Blondin.

The people in the crowd are asking many questions. Does Mr. Blondin see the white water under him? Will he fall? Is he **afraid**? Can he swim? Is the wind going to push him off the line?

Blondin walks across the line. He jumps. He runs. But he doesn't fall. He doesn't die. And he doesn't stop. Now Blondin wants to walk across again. He carries another man on his back. He walks across the line with his feet in bags. He doesn't rest.

Blondin goes to the middle of the line. He eats a piece of cake there. He drinks a glass of Niagara Falls water too.

---

imagine - make believe that something is true, pretend.
line - a long piece of rope or wire.
afraid - frightened, feeling fear.

Jean Blondin crossing
Niagara Falls on a
high line.
(Reproduced with
the permission of
the Niagara Falls,
New York Public
Library)

Then he **takes off** his hat and holds it out. The *Maid of the Mist* is under Blondin. On the ship, there is a man with a gun. The man makes a hole in Blondin's hat. Now Blondin is happy. He returns to the land and he rests.

In later years, other people try this. Some people do it well, and some people die. Some people go over the waterfall in a **barrel**. Mrs. Anna Edson Taylor is one of these people. She goes over Niagara Falls in a barrel on October 23, 1901. She lives, but she doesn't do it again.

Some animals go over Niagara Falls. They go over because they are not careful. Fish and water birds go over the waterfall. They die. You can go to the bottom of the waterfall and see many **dead** fish, birds, and other animals. It is sad.

There are green trees and big hills beside the waterfall. There are many happy animals. There are many happy people. Niagara Falls is a beautiful place, but it is a dangerous place too.

Mrs. Anna Edson Taylor after going over Niagara Falls in a barrel.
(Reproduced with the permission of the Niagara Falls, New York Public Library)

---

take off - remove.
barrel - a large, round container. A barrel is made of wood.
dead - not alive. An animal is dead after it dies.

Niagara Falls

A. Remembering facts. Which answer is NOT correct?

0. Under Niagara Falls, the water is very _______.
   a. white   b. cold   **c. dry**   d. fast

1. In summer, Niagara Falls is _______.

   a. fast   b. quiet   c. dangerous   d. cold

2. The *Maid of the Mist* goes _______.
   a. under   b. near   c. on white   d. over
      Niagara   Niagara   water   Niagara
      Falls   Falls   Falls

3. The walkway behind Niagara Falls is _______.
   a. wide   b. wet   c. narrow   d. light

4. Niagara Falls is quiet in _______.
   a. July   b. November   c. January   d. March

5. On the line across the river, Mr. Blondin _______.
   a. walks   b. jumps   c. runs   d. rests

B. Describing with color. In the story, what does each of these colors describe?

blue   milk-colored
brown   white
green   yellow

0. not slow, not fast rivers   blue

1. fast rivers   _______

2. slow rivers   _______

3. the water under Niagara Falls   _______

4. sunshine   _______

5. trees   _______

C. Word sets. Which word is different?

0.	Spanish	English	Chinese	**Canada**
1.	river	sun	rain	waterfall
2.	ice	cold	winter	swim
3.	son	woman	husband	wife
4.	England	Japan	Canadian	France
5.	noise	speak	hear	listen

D. Expanding sentences. Can you find the reason for each statement?

0. The Niagara River is white because
   (**e**) the water is fast and angry.

1. Ships don't use the Niagara River		a. the waterfall stops.
2. The Niagara River is dangerous		b. they want to die.
3. Niagara Falls is quiet in winter		c. the water is cold.
4. The weather at Niagara Falls is nice in summer (two reasons)	because	d. they are not careful.
5. Some people jump into the Niagara River		e. the water is fast and angry.
6. Mr. Blondin and Mrs. Taylor come to Niagara Falls		f. the river is dangerou
7. Some animals go over Niagara Falls		g. there is a lot of wate in the air.
		h. they like to do dangerous things.
		i. it becomes a waterfal

E. Word puzzle. (1) Use the letters in each box to make a word or words from the list; write the word(s) correctly. (2) Find the sentence about the words(s); write the number of the sentence in the circle. (3) Add the numbers across and the numbers down; the total will be 15 for each group of numbers.

BLONDIN	MAID OF THE MIST	THE UNITED STAT
CANADA	RAINBOW	WATERFALL
GET MARRIED	SWIM	WHITE

TEG MADIERR	LAFTERLAW	ADNAAC
(9)		= 15
GET MARRIED	___ ___	___
RABWINO	TWHIE	MIWS
		= 15
___	___	___
IDAM FO TEH STIM	EHT DENITU SETTAS	DINBLON
		= 15
___	___ ___	___
___		
= 15	= 15	= 15

1. This country is north of the U.S.
2. This boat goes under Niagara Falls.
3. The water in the Niagara River is this color.
4. Sunshine on rain or mist makes this.
5. Water goes down very quickly here.
6. He walks over Niagara Falls.
7. "The U.S." is a short way of writing this.
8. You can't do this in the Niagara River.
9. A man and woman can become husband and wife.

Fossils from the
Petrified Forest
National Monument,
Arizona. (Reproduced
with the permission
of the American
Museum of Natural
History)

The Grand Canyon: Books in Rocks

What kind of books can you find at the Grand Canyon?
What stories do they tell?
Who are the writers of these books?
How can people go down into the canyon to read the books?

1

The Colorado River is not a big river. It is long, but it is not big. But this little river is very strong and fast. It is not a blue or brown river. It is fast, so it is part white. It is part red, too. It is red because it cuts a lot of red **rocks**.

It cuts very deep into the red rock and ground under it. At one place, the Colorado River cuts into the rock for 217 miles (349 kilometers). It cuts it 4 to 18 miles (6.4 to 29 kilometers) across. It cuts it 1 mile (1.61 kilometers) into the ground. This place is called the Grand Canyon. This place is in the **southwestern** part of the U.S. It is a hot, dry place. It is near Mexico. It is important because it is a very old place.

---

rock (uncountable noun) - the solid, stony part of the earth. Compare *a rock* (countable noun). A rock is bigger than a stone.
southwestern -

The Grand Canyon is **10,000,000** years old. Many other places in the world have old rocks. But the old rocks in the Grand Canyon are open. You can see them very well. They are open rock-books. These books have many stories for us. They have stories about the rocks of the world, the plants of the world, and the animals of the world. These rock-books don't have paper pages. **Nobody** writes them. They don't have English words. But people can read them.

2

You can read the stories in the rocks. Look at the picture (page 15) of the rocks of the Grand Canyon. See the lines that go across the rocks. The lines are wide or narrow, and they are every color. Every line is **different**. The rocks and the lines are different because they are different ages.

The rocks on the walls of the high part of the Grand Canyon are young. The rocks in the middle part are old. The

---

10,000,000 - ten million.
nobody - no one, no person.
different - not the same. In the letters aaaAa, A is different.

14

(Opposite) Colorado River, foot of the Red Canyon Trail, Grand Canyon. (Above) The rock walls of the Grand Canyon, view from Bright Angel Point. (Reproduced with the permission of the Arizona Historical Society)

rocks on the bottom are as old as the world.

You can read the plant and animal stories. There are fossils in the rock walls of the canyon. Fossils are old, dry, plants and animals in rocks. People can look at the top walls and see young fossils. They can look at the middle walls and see old fossils. They can look at the bottom walls and see very old fossils. The Grand Canyon is a good storyteller because it tells the right age for every rock and fossil.

3

The Colorado River writes a new page in the books of the Grand Canyon every day. But the river is not the only writer. The wind helps a lot, too. The wind carries sand and **dirt** and cuts the rocks. The rain is another writer. It doesn't rain often in the Grand Canyon; but in summer, it can rain a lot in one day. The rain water falls very fast over the open rock. It cuts the rocks, too. In winter, ice comes. It can push

---

dirt - earth, soil. Plants grow in dirt. Compare *dirty*, not clean. City streets are often dirty.

the rocks open and break them. The Colorado River is the best writer, but it has three helpers: the wind, the rain, and the ice.

4

People from every part of the world come to visit the Grand Canyon. Some people come here to study the rocks, the river, or the fossils. But most people come here to look at the beautiful rocks and the river. The air is very clean here. People can stand at the top of the Grand Canyon and see the other side. They can see many miles or kilometers. They can see the river, one mile down.

Other people like to walk down into the canyon. The walkers must be very careful. Walking down into the canyon is not easy, and it is dangerous. The red Colorado River water is dirty, so they can't drink it. There aren't any stairs, so they can't walk down easily. There are only narrow, dirty walkways. It gets very hot in the canyon. It can be 125°F (51.5°C). Walkers get very thirsty. They must carry a lot of water.

Some people don't like to walk, but they still want to go down into the canyon. There aren't any roads, so they can't drive a car. But they can ride on animals called **mules**. Mules don't like to carry heavy people. They like to play with people. They like to walk near the side of the walkway. They like to go down dangerous ways. The people become afraid. But the mules don't fall. They walk very well here.

---

mule - a mule is half-horse, half-donkey. See picture, page 17.

Coming down the Grand View Trail, Trail, Grand Canyon. (Reproduced with the permission of the Arizona Historical Society)

Mules are not the only animals in the Grand Canyon. **Mountain** sheep live here too. These sheep can walk on the mountains and high rocks. They can jump up very high and walk very carefully. They don't need walkways, roads, or stairs. They are quiet, and they live in quiet places.

High over the canyon, you can see eagles. This large, strong bird can fly over the mountains. Eagles eat other birds and small animals. They are the U.S. bird. You can see them on U.S. money and stamps.

---

mountain - a high place on earth bigger than a hill. The Grand Canyon is near the Rocky Mountains.

Eagle after an osprey, a kind of hawk. (Reproduced with the permission of the American Museum of Natural History)

5

The Grand Canyon is a big, beautiful, quiet place. Many people see **God** here. Many people like to talk to God here. Parts of the canyon have the names of gods and goddesses from other parts of the world. Some names are from old Greece and Rome: Venus Temple, Jupiter Temple, Apollo Butte. Other names are from Egypt: Isis Temple, Horus Temple, Osiris Temple. Other names are from India: Shiva Temple, Buddha Temple, Brahma Temple.

Come to the Grand Canyon. Count the lines and years in the rocks. Look at the fossils. Ride the mules. Watch the river, rain, wind, and ice cut the canyon. Read the beautiful story of time in the rock-books.

God - the Supreme Being. People talk to God in church. Compare *god, goddess.*

The Grand Canyon

A. Remember or look back. Use information from the story to answer these questions.

0. The Colorado River is white and red. Why is it white? **Because it is very fast. Fast rivers are white.**

1. Why is the Colorado River red?

2. Where is the Grand Canyon?

3. What kind of books can you find at the Grand Canyon?

4 What stories do they tell?

5. Who writes these stories?

6. How can people go down into the Grand Canyon to read the rock-books?

B. Pointing words. Look at these sentences from the story. What word does each of the words in dark type point back to?

0. At one place, the Colorado River cuts into the rock for 217 miles. **It** cuts **it** 4 to 18 miles across.
   It—the Colorado River; it—the rock

1. These rock-books don't have paper pages. Nobody writes **them**. **They** don't have English words.

2. In winter, ice comes. **It** can push the rocks open and break **them**.

3. The walkers must be very careful. The red Colorado River water is dirty, so **they** can't drink **it**.

C. Make a choice. Choose the correct word for each space.

0. carry, carries
   Walkers in the Grand Canyon must carry water.
   Every walker carries it.

1. fly, flies
   Eagles _______ over the Grand Canyon.
   An eagle _______ to look for food.

2. story, stories
   The rocks of the Canyon tell three _______.
   One _______ is about the rocks of the world.
   The other _______ are about the plants and animals of the world.

D. Crossword puzzle. There is one space in the puzzle for each letter. Match the definitions with the spaces. All of the words are from the first two stories. To help you, 1-down and 22-across are already done. For this puzzle, you may want to work with a friend.

<table>
<tr><td valign="top">

Across

2. A __ writes.
6. Sheep or mule
9. Come __ the Grand
   Canyon.
10. 1.5 = one and a __
12. Not the same
15. Not before
18. Old, dry plants or
   animals in rocks
21. Venus or Horus __
22. Rock-books place
23. Not safe
24. Go over Niagara
   Falls in this.
26. __ down into the
   Grand Canyon.
28. Ride __ a mule.
29. Sunshine through
   rain makes this.
32. Not over
34. Some people can't
   __ at night.
35. Use a language
36. Good on rocks
37. Not up

</td><td valign="top">

Down

1. A big waterfall
2. Water falls here.
3. __ is hot in summer.
4. Not the bottom
5. __ in a car.
7. Water in winter
8. Blondin walks on a __.
11. Mules don't like __ people.
13. 3 __ = 0.91 meters
14. It's not __ to walk
   in the Grand Canyon.
16. For your finger
17. Make believe, pretend
19. Not off
20. There aren't any roads,
   __ you can't drive a car.
25. It can cut through rock.
26. People talk to __ in
   a temple.
27. The number before *two*
30. Blondin is not __ .
31. People live in every part
   of the __ .
32. Not down
33. Stop working
36. Not a woman

</td></tr>
</table>

E. Finish the paragraph. Choose the correct word for each
space. Use each word once.

at, at, at, at, behind, from, into, of, of, on, on, through

Every year people come **from** every part   (1) the world
to visit Niagara Falls and the Grand Canyon.   (2) Niagara
Falls they can walk   (3) the waterfall and see the
sunshine   (4) a water window. They can ride   (5) the
Maid   (6) *the Mist*.   (7) the Grand Canyon, the people
can look   (8) open rock-books. They can walk down
(9) the canyon. They can ride   (10) mules. There is a
lot to do   (11) the two places.

HERE 1475 FT.
ABOVE
THE OCEAN
THE MIGHTY
MISSISSIPPI
BEGINS
TO FLOW
ON ITS
WINDING WAY
2552 MILES
TO THE
GULF
OF MEXICO

The Mississippi: River of Many Names

Where is the Mississippi River?
Why is it important?
What are some of its names?

1

The Niagara River is white. The Colorado River is red. The Mississippi River is brown. It is slow, but it is long, strong, and important.

The Mississippi is 2,380 miles (3,780 kilometers) long. It is a long water roadway. It starts near Canada. Then it goes through the flat farmland in the center of the U.S. Then it goes into the Gulf of Mexico in the southern U.S.

Big ships can go on the Mississippi River. They can carry many things on this water roadway. They can carry **iron** and wood from the northern U.S. They can carry food from the farms in the center of the U.S. They can carry **oil** and **cotton** from the southern U.S. The ships carry all of these things to New Orleans. Other ships take the iron, wood, food, oil, and cotton from New Orleans to every part of the world. The Mississippi is a water roadway for the world.

---

iron - the most common metal. Its symbol is Fe.
oil - an important black liquid. It comes from the ground. It is also called petroleum.
cotton - the soft, white part of the cotton plant. In summer, people wear cotton clothes.

Mississippi riverboats.
(Reproduced with the permission
of the National Archives)

2

Mississippi is an American Indian word for "Big River." That is a good name for the river, but it is not the only name.

Some people call the Mississippi the "Father of All **Waters**." That is a good name, too. The river carries water from many other big rivers in the U.S. and Canada. The Missouri River is one of these big rivers. It is 2,565 miles (4,130 kilometers) long, but it doesn't go to the sea. It needs the Mississippi to do that. A lot of land gives its water to the river. Part of New York State gives its water from the east. Part of Canada gives its water from the north. From the west, the Rocky Mountains give some of their water. All of this land pushes its rain and **snow** water into the Mississippi.

---

waters - lakes or rivers.
snow - Snow falls in winter. It is cold and white.

3

Another name for the Mississippi is "Old Man River."* Old Man River sleeps on a bed. The bed is the bottom of the river. But the river doesn't sleep quietly on this bed. In spring, the land gives a lot of rainwater to the river. Then the Mississippi floods. It goes up very high and out very wide. It goes everywhere. It goes over farms. It goes over streets and cars. It goes up the sides of buildings. Sometimes the river breaks the buildings. Then you can see pieces of houses in the water. Some people lose their houses, their cars, and their land. They call the river the "**Mighty** Mississippi."

In some places, people stop this mighty river. They build high, strong walls on the side of the river. These walls are called levees. The river can't flood the land there. With levees, the people aren't afraid of the Mighty Mississippi.

Without levees, the Mississippi can move to the side. It can change its bed. Sometimes it can move in one night. A farmer has a big farm. He goes to sleep one night. Then the river moves. The next morning, the farmer gets up. The river has a new bed: his farm! His farm is under the Mississippi, and he can't do anything.

The land beside the Mississippi pushes a lot of dirt into the river. This soft, wet dirt is called mud. There is a lot of mud in the river, so some people call the Mississippi the "Big Muddy." The mud isn't beautiful, but it is important. The river is full of mud. The mud has good food for plants. In spring the river floods. This flooding puts the good mud on the farms. So some farmers lose their farms to the Mississippi, and other farmers get good mud for their fields from the river.

---

*There is a song by Jerome Kern called "Old Man River." The song is from the musical comedy *Show Boat*.
mighty - very strong.

Another name for the river is "Old Miss." The Mississippi is really very old. It is 12,000,000 years old. Some towns on the Mississippi are 250 years old. The U.S. is 200 years old. People in the U.S. like to talk about the "old days" on the Mississippi—100 years **ago**. People read about these old days in the stories of Mark Twain. Many people say, "Mark Twain is the best American author." Two of his books are *The Adventures of Tom Sawyer* and *Huckleberry Finn*. In these books, boys play and live on the old Mississippi. They run away from home. They go down the river on a **raft**. They eat **catfish**. They sleep on an **island**. They meet some good people and some bad people. Many American boys want to be Tom Sawyer or Huckleberry Finn.

The Mississippi, the Father of All Waters, Old Man River, the Mighty Mississippi, the Big Muddy, Old Miss —these are six names for one big river.

---

ago - before the present.
raft - a flat boat without sides.
catfish - a fish with long hairs on its face. People say it looks like a cat.
island - a piece of land with water all around it.

The Mississippi

. Remember or look back. Here are four sentences about the Mississippi. Can you find the answers to each of the questions?

0. Some people call the Mississippi the "Father of All Waters."
    a. What does *waters* mean?
       Lakes or rivers.
    b. Why is "Father of All Waters" a good name for the Mississippi?
       Because many rivers give their water to the Mississippi.

1. Some people call the Mississippi the "Mighty Mississippi."
    a. What does *mighty* mean?
    b. Why is this a good name for the river?

2. Some people call the Mississippi the "Big Muddy."
    a. What does *muddy* mean?
    b. Why is this a good name for the river?

3. The Mississippi is slow, but it is long, strong, and important.
    a. How long is it?
    b. How strong is it?
    c. Why is it important?

B. Spelling help. Look carefully at each pair of words. Then try to write the words without looking at this page.

0. w o o_	w_ _ _d	**wood**
1. c o_ _o_	c_t t_n	
2. f_o o_	f l_ _ _d	
3. n a_u_a_	n_t_r_l	
4. N i a_a_a	N_ _g_r_	
5. M i_ _i_ _i_ _i	M_s s_s s_p p_	

C. Picture that. The word *Mississippi* has many s's. The Mississippi River does, too. Sometimes there are two towns on the river. One town is on one S-shape. The other town is on another S-shape. A bird can go between the two towns by flying 5 miles (8 kilometers). A boat can go between the two towns, too. But the boat must go 30 miles (48 kilometers).
Show the bird's way to go between them. Show the boat's way.

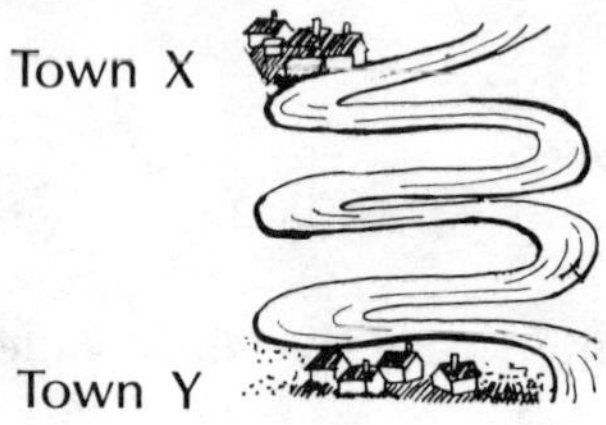

D. Finish the paragraph. Can you guess the missing words? You have some letters to help you.

Many big fish live in the m_d d y Mississippi. One of these f_s_ can be 9 f__t (2.75 meters) long. Its teeth a_e very dangerous. It _s called a gar. Another b_g fish is c__l_d a catfish. It has __ cat face. A big Mississippi c_t f_s_ can weigh 150 pounds (70 kilograms). Many small catfish l_v_ in the __s s_s s_p p_, too. Catfish are g__d to eat.

E. Your ideas. Answer these questions, then talk about your answers.

1. What important river do you know? Why is it important? What color is it?
2. Are there boats and ships on it? If so, what do they carry?
3. Do people have many names for this river? If so, what are some of them?
4. Are there farms near the river? If so, what grows there?
5. Are there towns near the river? If so, how old are they?
6. Do you think 250 years is very old for a town? Do you think 200 years is very old for a country? If not, how old is "old" for you?

Statue of Tom
Sawyer and
Huckleberry Finn.
(Reproduced with
the permission of
the Missouri
Historical Society)

Riverside Geyser,
Yellowstone National
Park. (Reproduced
with the permission
of the National
Archives)

Yellowstone National Park: Strange Water

*Why is the water at Yellowstone National Park **strange**?*
You can see strange water at Yellowstone. What else can you see there?
How can you visit Yellowstone?

1

Yellowstone National Park is a big place. Its shape is a square. The park is 60 miles (96 kilometers) wide and 60 miles long. Yellowstone is a natural place. In the park, nobody can **kill** the animals. Nobody can cut down the trees. Nobody can take away the rocks. Nobody can take the water for farms. Nobody can make it different because it is a national park.

Yellowstone has everything. It has lakes, rivers, and waterfalls. It has mountains, canyons, and big rocks. It has many big animals and many tall trees. Yes, other places have these things, too. But Yellowstone has something different. It has hot water. This water comes out of the ground and does strange things.

strange - surprising, hard to understand.
kill - make something die, take away life.

2

Water comes out of the ground in a place called a **spring**. Mammoth Hot Springs is an example. (Its picture is on the cover of this book.) Mammoth Hot Springs is a place of water and rocks. The Grand Canyon is a place of water and rocks, too. In the Grand Canyon, the water cuts down into the rock. But the water at Mammoth Hot Springs is different. It helps the rock grow!

The hot springs are always growing. They grow because there are very, very small pieces of rock in the water. These rock pieces can stay in hot water, but they can't stay in cold water. The water under the ground is very hot, so the rock pieces stay in the water there. But then the hot water brings these very, very small pieces up from the ground. Out of the ground, the air is not hot. The water becomes **less** hot. The rock pieces fall to the bottom of the water. They stay on the other rocks. They make a big rock stairway. But you can't walk up the stairway because very hot water is going down.

3

Some hot springs send up a tall, thin cloud of hot water and **steam**. These springs are called geysers. Old Faithful geyser is an example. People come to watch Old Faithful. First, they must wait for it. They go to a large empty field. There is a hole in the ground. The hole is ten feet wide. No trees or plants grow near it. Under the ground, there are

---

spring - water coming up from the ground.
less - not as much, smaller in amount.
steam - Water turns to steam at 212° F (100° C).

strange **loud** noises. Some people are afraid. They go away. The air is very bad. Some people hold their noses because they don't want to **smell** the air. Everybody waits. Then, BOOM! There is a loud noise. Steam and hot water come up from the hole. The geyser is very hot, quick, and strong. The steam and hot water go up 150 feet (46 meters) into the air. Then Old Faithful is quiet. One hour later, the water goes up again. Old Faithful rests for an hour, then it shows its tall hot water and steam again. It is always faithful.

Old Faithful,
Yellowstone National
Park. (Courtesy of
the United States
National Park Service)

---

loud - not quiet. "BOOM!" shows a loud noise.
smell - what you do with your nose.

4

There is cold water, too, in Yellowstone. It is in the Yellowstone River. The river is like the springs and the geysers—it is very strange. Some parts of the river have hot water. People like to swim there. They can swim in those parts of the river in summer or winter. The air is very cold, but the water is always hot.

There are many fish in the river. People like to catch fish in the cold parts of the river. Some people want to eat the fish right away. They don't want to wait. So they cook the fish in the river! They take the fish to a hot part of the river and put it into the hot water. The hot water cooks it. Then the people take the fish out and eat it.

5

There are many big animals in Yellowstone. People like the **bears** best. The bears are funny. They stand on two legs and ask for food. People like to give them food, but it is dangerous. The police in the park say, "Do not feed the bears!" Some people feed baby bears. They play with them. Then their mother comes, and she becomes very angry. She has big teeth, too. Sometimes angry bears eat people. The park police say, "Stay in your cars. Put up your windows. Close your doors. Watch the bears and take their picture, but don't feed them!"

There are big **bison** here, too. They are very big and heavy. They are 6 feet (1.8 meters) tall at the **shoulder**. The

---

bear - a large wild animal. See picture, page 35.
bison - This animal is also called a buffalo. See picture, page 35.
shoulder - A person's arm (or an animal's front leg) joins the body here.

bison eat grass and drink water in the flat, quiet part of Yellowstone. But they become afraid sometimes. They run then. They make a very loud noise. The ground moves. There is dirt in the air. People run away from them. It is nice to watch the animals at Yellowstone, but you must be careful. They are a little bit dangerous.

Bears (left) and bison (below) at Yellowstone National Park. (Courtesy of the United States National Park Service)

6

There are two ways to visit Yellowstone. You can stay in a hotel, or you can go **camping**. The best way to see Yellowstone is to go camping. That way, you can sleep under the moon and the stars. You can sit beside a fire at night. You can sing with your friends. You can listen to the waterfalls and the geysers.

---

camping - sleeping under the stars, out of a house.

Cornelius Hedges.
(Courtesy of the
United States
National Park Service)

Some people want to take the park for themselves. They want to make a lot of money from the visitors. But it is a national park, so they can't. It is the first national park in the U.S. or the world. Here is its story.

Imagine it is 1872. The first white men are visiting Yellowstone. They are going camping here. They are sitting beside a fire. One man is talking.

He says, "This is a beautiful place. Many people will want to visit here. They will pay a lot of money. Let's take this place for us. Let's make it our place. I will take Old Faithful. You can take Mammoth Hot Springs, Tom. Samuel, you can take the waterfalls, and, James, you can take the rivers. We will make big hotels here. We will make a lot of money!"

"Yes! We will all be rich!" Tom says.

"Wait a minute." Cornelius Hedges is talking. He says, "This isn't good. Let's make a park. Let's give it to the people of the U.S. It will be a national park. It will be free. People will come from everywhere. Rich people will see the park, but other people will, too."

"That's better," the men say. "We won't be rich, but we will be happy because everybody will be able to see the park."

Today people say "thank you" to Cornelius Hedges. Because of him, the park is open to everybody.

Yellowstone National Park

A. Time order. According to the story, what happens first at Old Faithful? What happens next? Number the sentences to show the correct order.

___ There are strange noises under the ground.

___ Some people hold their noses because the air is very bad.

___ Steam and hot water go up 150 feet into the air.

1 People come to watch.

___ BOOM! There is a big noise.

___ Some people are afraid and go away.

B. Lookalikes. Choose the correct word.

0. You can (cake/**cook**) a fish in the Yellowstone River.

1. It isn't good to give (food/wood) to a (bear/beer).

2. You must (wait/white) one hour for Old Faithful.

3. Bison like to eat (glass/grass).

4. Old Faithful makes strange (noises/noses).

5. People like to go camping and sleep under the (stairs/stars).

C. Finish the outline. Fill in the missing words in this outline. You have one space for each letter.

0. Yellowstone Park is sixty miles square.

1. In a national park, nobody can
   a. k__l the animals,
   b. __k_ _w_y the rocks, or
   c. __k_ the water for farms.

2. Yellowstone National Park has
   a. l_k_s, rivers, and w_t_r_a_l_;
   b. mountains, __ny___, and big rocks;
   c. big animals and _r_e_; and
   d. _o_ __t_r.

3. The hot water comes out of the ground in three ways:
   a. s_r__g_ (like Mammoth Hot
      S_r__g_),
   b. g_ys__s (like Old Faithful), and
   c. a r____r (the Yellowstone R____r).

4. People go fishing there in a strange way.
   a. They catch the fish in the _o__ part of the Yellowstone River.
   b. Then they take the fish to the _o_ part of the river.
   c. The hot water __o__ the fish.
   d. Then the people _a_ the fish.

5. Two kinds of big and dangerous animals in the park are
   a. b____s and
   b. b___n.

6. Two ways to visit the park are to
   a. _t_y in a h_t__ or
   b. g_ c__p__g.

. Word sets. Add the appropriate words.

0. hot:summer :: cold:**winter**

1. day:sun :: night:___

2. food:mouth :: air:___

3. eat:grass :: drink:___

4. mountain:high :: canyon:___

Sentence completion. Finish these sentences. Use ideas from the story. There are several possible answers for each one.

0. It is nice to watch the animals at
   Yellowstone, but | you must be careful.
                    | some of the animals are dangerous.
                    | don't feed the bears.

1. In some parts of the Yellowstone River, the water is hot in winter, so...

2. People like to feed the bears, but...

3. At Yellowstone Park, you can stay in a hotel or...

4. "We will make big hotels here and..."

5. Now everyone can see Yellowstone Park because...

El Capitan, Yosemite
National Park.
(Reproduced with
the permission of
the California
Historical Society)

Yosemite National Park: The Glaciers' Stories

What is a glacier?
How does it tell a story?
What can a visitor see and do in Yosemite Park?

1

Rivers can cut rocks. Wind and rain can cut rocks. But they aren't the only rock-cutters. Glaciers can cut rocks too. Glaciers are ice rivers. They move very slowly, but they are very strong. Their work needs a lot of time. It is not easy, but it is beautiful. The glaciers cut high places and low places. They make round rocks and square rocks. They make flat glass rocks. They write on the rocks.

At Yosemite National Park, the glaciers are finished. You can come and see their work. You can see high mountains and low **valleys**. You can see very tall white waterfalls. You can see round rocks and flat rocks. Between the rocks, you can see very large trees. You can see big animals. Many people say, "This is the best place in the Unites States. All the best natural things are in Yosemite National Park."

---

valleys - A valley is a low, flat place between hills or mountains.

2

Yosemite Valley is one small part of the park, but it is the best part. There are many big mountains on the sides of the valley: Three Brothers, **El Capitan**, and Half Dome. They are 2,000 to 4,800 feet (600 to 1,460 meters) high. They stand up over the flat valley.

Three Brothers are three mountains side by side. El Capitan has tall, flat sides. Half Dome is half round and half flat. It is a big half ball. These mountains all show the glaciers' work.

Half Dome, Yosemite National Park. (Reproduced with the permission of the California Historical Society)

El Capitan - This name is Spanish; it means "the captain."

Some people **climb** up the side of Half Dome and El Capitan. They climb up the wall to the sky. They need strong lines. They must make holes in the rock. They put their fingers in the holes. They must not be afraid. They must not fall. They must climb carefully.

3

There are waterfalls between the mountains. Niagara Falls is a very high waterfall. But three waterfalls at Yosemite are very, very high. At Yosemite Falls, water falls 2,425 feet (739 meters). It is the highest waterfall in North America. It is narrow, so the wind moves it. You can listen to the waterfall meet the rocks at the bottom. The noise is loud one minute, then it is quiet the next minute. There is a lot of mist in the air, so the sun makes beautiful rainbows here. The moon makes night rainbows too.

The best time for waterfalls in Yosemite is in spring, in May and June. In spring, the winter snow and ice become water under the hot sun and the blue sky. All the rivers are full. The waterfalls are strong. But summer dries many of the waterfalls. They are quiet in summer, autumn, and winter.

Some nights people make a fire-fall. They make a big, hot fire at the top of a waterfall. Then, they push the fire into the water. It makes a strange, orange light all the way down the waterfall. There is a line of orange in the black night. But some people don't like this fire-fall because it isn't natural. "Let's keep Yosemite natural," they say.

The water from all these waterfalls goes down into the Merced River. This river goes through the middle of the valley. It is a clean, blue little river. People like to swim here. It has fish. People catch fish here, too.

---

climb - go up a mountain, a tree, or stairs.

Merced River, Yosemite National Park. (Reproduced with the permission of the California Historical Society)

4

Yosemite National Park is not only Yosemite Valley. There are many other nice places here. There are other mountains, valleys, and waterfalls. There are no other fire-falls, but there are animals. There are mountain sheep, bears, and deer. People try to be quiet; then the animals don't run away.

It is nice to walk in Yosemite. Some people go camping here for many days. They smell the trees and flowers and the clean air. They listen to the waterfalls and to the wind in the trees. They watch the animals. They see the snow on top of the mountains. They walk across the mountains and valleys.

Other people ride horses in Yosemite. The people like it, and the horses do too. The horses can't walk on the dangerous rock mountains. They are not mules. But they can go to the other places. People can ride bicycles, too. They can go camping here, or they can stay in a hotel and sleep in a bed.

There are many large trees at Yosemite. It is a national park, so no one can cut them. They are very big and old. Yosemite Valley has many of them. But 35 miles (56 kilometers) south of Yosemite Valley, there are really large trees. They are called sequoias. Many sequoias are 200 feet (61 meters) tall. The king of the sequoias is called the **Grizzly Giant**. It has a **diameter** of 35 feet (11 meters). Its **circumference** is 96 feet (29 meters). It is large, and it is really old, too. It is 3,800 years old. Under the sequoia trees, it is very quiet. Cars cannot come here. People are quiet. They don't want to talk here. The trees are very big, and the people are very small.

Yosemite has big trees. It has smooth rock walls. It has the strange rock shapes of the glaciers. It has waterfalls. It has flowers and animals. It has the best parts of nature in one place. Come and see these beautiful places. Remember them. They are here for you.

Grizzly Giant, Mariposa Grove, Yosemite National Park. (Reproduced with the permission of the California Historical Society)

Grizzly Giant - the name of a tree.
  grizzly - from *grizzled*, with gray hair.
  giant - a very big man, animal, or plant.
diameter - the distance across a circle.
circumference - the distance around a circle.

Yosemite National Park

A. Saying things different ways. Can you find the sentences in the story that say the same thing as these sentences?

0. The rivers have a lot of water in them.
   The rivers are full.

1. Glaciers tell stories.

2. You can't see a glacier now at Yosemite Park.

3. The Merced River isn't very fast, and it isn't very slow.

4. The visitors to Yosemite Park like to watch animals.

5. The Grizzly Giant is the name of the biggest sequoia tree in Yosemite Park.

6. Glaciers can change the shapes of high mountains. (four sentences)

B. Extra words. In this paragraph from the story, there is one extra word in each sentence. Can you find the seven extra words and cross them out? The first one is done as an example.

Some nights trees, people make a fire-fall. They make a big, hot fire to at the top of a waterfall. Then, they up push the fire into the water. It does makes a strange, orange light all the way down the waterfall. There is a line Tuesday of orange in the black night. But some people don't like this camping fire-fall because it isn't natural. "Let's keep Yosemite natural," they animal say.

C. Picture that. Can you identify each of these nine natural wonders?

1. **Niagara Falls**   4.   7.
2.   5.   8.
3.   6.   9.

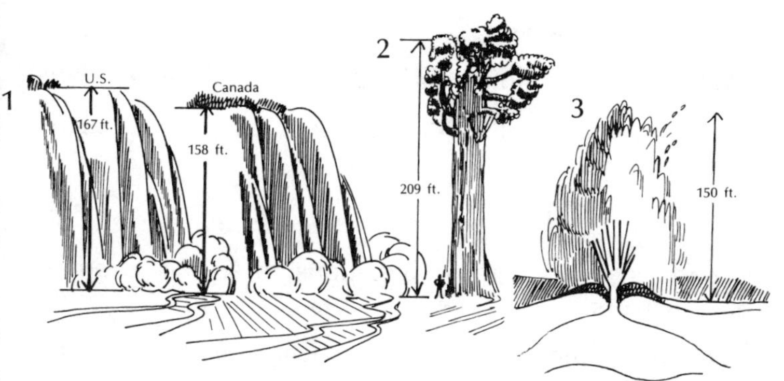

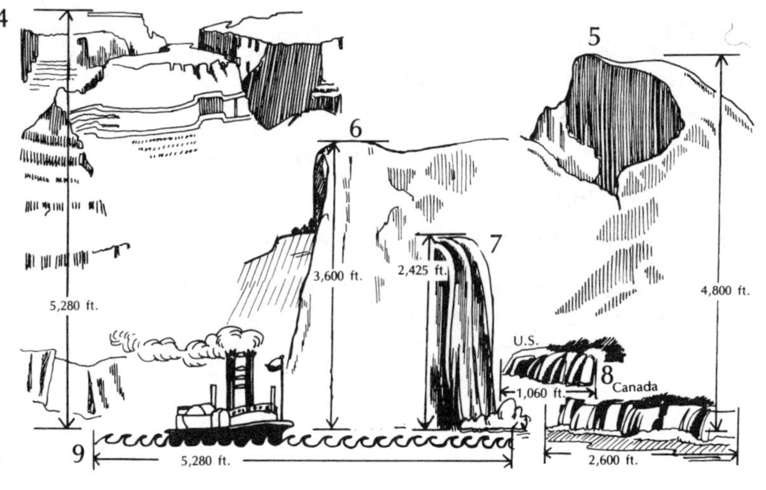

D. Test your memory. Where do these animals live? List
each of them in the correct place. (Some animals live in
two places.)

      bear, bison, catfish, deer, eagle,
      gar, horse, mule, mountain sheep

1. The Mississippi River: ___gar___, ________

2. The Grand Canyon: ________, ________, ________

3. Yellowstone National Park: ________, ________

4. Yosemite National Park: ________, ________, ________,
____

E. Your ideas. Answer these questions; then talk about
your answers.

1. Is there a mountain or valley near your home? What
is it like? Is it green? Is it beautiful?

2. Where do you see rainbows? Do you like them?
Why?

3. Do you or your friends go camping? Do you like to
walk in the mountains? Why?

4. Do you live near a large tree or animal? Is it old? Is
it important to you? Why?

5. Can you ride a horse? Does the horse like it?

6. Do you know about other natural wonders in the
world? Can you describe one?

Answer Key

One   Niagara Falls

A. 1. b   2. d   3. a   4. a   5. d
B. 1. white 2. brown 3. milk-colored 4. yellow 5. green
C. 1. sun 2. swim 3. woman 4. Canadian 5. noise
D. 1. f   2. i   3. a   4. c and g   5. b   6. h   7. d

①	②	③
GET MARRIED	WATERFALL	CANADA
④	⑤	⑥
RAINBOW	WHITE	SWIM
⑦	⑧	⑨
MAID OF THE MIST	THE UNITED STATES	BLONDIN

A. 1. Because it cuts red rocks. The pieces of rock make it red.
   2. In the southwestern part of the U.S. It is near Mexico.
   3. Open rock-books.
   4. Stories about the rocks, plants, and animals of the world.
   5. The Colorado River and its three helpers. The three helpers are the wind, the rain, and the ice.
   6. They can walk down, or they can ride on mules.

B. 1. them, They-these rock books.
   2. It-ice; them-the rocks.
   3. they-the walkers; it-the red Colorado River water.

C. 1. fly; flies   2. stories; story; stories

D.

E. 1. of 2. At 3. behind 4. through 5. on
   6. *of* 7. At 8. at 9. into 10. on 11. at

Three   The Mississippi

A. 1. a. Very strong.
   b. The river can flood farms and towns. It can break buildings. It can move to the side.
2. a. Full of soft, wet dirt.
   b. The river carries a lot of mud.
3. a. It is 2,565 miles (4,130 kilometers) long.
   b. It is very strong. (See 1.b for examples of how strong it is.)
   c. It is a water roadway for the world, and it puts good mud on farms.

B. 1. cotton   2. flood   3. natural   4. Niagara
   5. Mississippi

C.

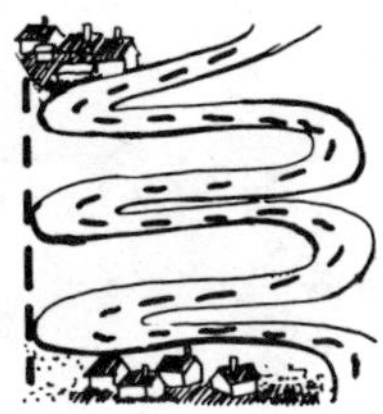

D. Many big fish live in the <u>muddy</u> Mississippi. One of these <u>fish</u> can be 9 <u>feet</u> (2.75 meters) long. Its teeth <u>are</u> very dangerous. It <u>is</u> called a gar. Another <u>big</u> fish is <u>called</u> a catfish. It has <u>a</u> cat face. A big Mississippi <u>catfish</u> can weigh 150 pounds (70 kilograms). Many small catfish <u>live</u> in the <u>Mississippi</u>, too. Catfish are <u>good</u> to eat.
Individual answers.

Four   Yellowstone National Park

A. 2, 4, 6, 1, 5, 3

B. 1. food, bear 2. wait 3. grass 4. noises
5. stars

C. 1. a. kill b. take away c. take
2. a. lakes, waterfalls b. canyons c. trees d. hot water
3. a. springs, Springs b. geysers c. river, River
4. a. cold b. hot c. cooks d. eat
5. a. bears b. bison (buffalo)
6. a. stay, hotel b. go camping

D. 1. moon 2. nose 3. water 4. deep

E. 1. people swim there/you can go swimming in winter.
2. it is dangerous/the park police tell people, "Don't feed the bears."
3. you can go camping/you can sleep under the stars.
4. make a lot of money/become rich.
5. it is free/it is a national park.

Five   Yosemite National Park

A. 1. They write on the rocks.
2. At Yosemite National Park, the glaciers are finished.
3. It is a clean, blue little river.
4. People try to be quiet; then the animals don't run away.
5. The king of the sequoias is called the Grizzly Giant.
6. Three Brothers are three mountains side by side. El Capitan has tall, flat sides. Half Dome is half round and half flat. These mountains all show the glaciers' work.

B. to, up, does, Tuesday, camping, animal

C. 1. Niagara Falls 2. the Grizzly Giant 3. Old Faithful 4. the Grand Canyon 5. Half Dome 6. El Capitan 7. Yosemite Falls 8. Niagara Falls 9. the Mississippi River

D. The Mississippi River: gar, catfish
The Grand Canyon: mule, eagle, mountain sheep
Yellowstone National Park: bear, bison
Yosemite National Park: bear, horse, deer, mountain sheep

E. Individual answers.